The world is full of poetry.

J. G. PERCIVAL
C. 1822

Little by Little – Signs of Learning®

*Dedicated with love to my grandchildren,
Sam III, Kate, Megan, and Mary,
From Grandmother Beth (Grandma).*

*For my best-loved grandchildren,
Ben, Henry, Isabelle, James, and Murray III,
for always and forever,
From Grandmother Mary Belle (oma-omee-mem)*

Registered Title: Murray David Harwich III

Text ©2017 Mary Belle Harwich

Illustrations ©2017 Beth Bird

ASL Illustrations ©2018 Rosalee Anderson

ALL RIGHTS RESERVED

Printed in the United States

Published Frankfort, KY

Book Designs by Marjorie Snelson Design

ISBN 978-0-9888972-6-7

Library of Congress Control Number: 2019913718

To order printed books: www.amazon.com

Little by Little
Poetry for Young Children

Signs of Learning®

Poem Selections and Text by Mary Belle Harwich

Illustrations by Beth Bird

ASL Illustrations by Rosalee Anderson

For You

I

Hats off!

Along the street there comes

A blare of bugles, a ruffle of drums,

A flash of color beneath the sky:

Hats off!

The flag is passing by!

II

I wake in the morning early,

And always the very first thing,

I poke out my head

And I sit up in bed

And I sing and I sing,

And I sing!

III

The friendly cow all red and white,

I love with all my heart:

She gives me cream with all her might,

To eat with apple-tart.

IV

If you were a bird, and lived on high,

You'd lean on the wind when the wind came by,

You'd say to the wind when it took you away:

That's where I wanted to go today!

V

How do you like to go up in a swing,

Up in the air so blue?

Oh, I do think it the pleasantest thing

Ever a child can do!

VI

Big red sugar plums are clinging

To the cliffs beside the sea

Where the Dinky-bird is singing

In the amfulula tree!

VII

Oh, there once was a puffin

Just the shape of a muffin,

And he lived on an island

In the

bright

blue sea!

VIII

Something told the wild geese

It was time to go,

Though the fields lay golden

Something whispered, "snow"

IX

Spades take up leaves

No better than spoons

And bags full of leaves

Are light as balloons

X

Whose woods these are I think I know.

His house is in the village though;

He will not see me stopping here

To watch his woods fill up with snow.

XI

I keep six honest serving-men;

They taught me all I knew.

Their names are What and Where and When

And How and Why and Who

XII

Thunder crashes.

Lightning flashes.

Rain makes puddles

So I can make splashes

XIII

By day you cannot see the sky

For it is up so very high.

You look and look, but it's so blue

That you can never see right through.

But when the night comes it is quite plain,

And all the stars are there again.

XIV

In jumping and tumbling

We spend the whole day,

Till night by arriving

Has finished our play.

What then? One and all,

There's no more to be said,

As we tumbled all day,

So we tumble to bed.

XV

The world is so full of a number of things

I'm sure we should all be as happy as kings

I

PAGE 8

The Flag Goes By
by Henry Holcomb Bennett

II

PAGE 10

Singing Time
by Rose Fyleman

III

PAGE 12

The Cow
by Robert Louis Stevenson

IV

PAGE 14

Spring Morning
by A.A. Milne

V

PAGE 16

The Swing
by Robert Louis Stevenson

VI

PAGE 18

The Dinky Bird
by Eugene Field

VII

PAGE 20

The Puffin
by Florence Page Jaques

VIII

PAGE 22

The Geese
by Rachel Field

IX

PAGE 24

Gathering Leaves
by Robert Frost

X

PAGE 26

Whose Woods These Are
by Robert Frost

XI

PAGE 28

Six Serving Men
by Rudyard kipling

XII

PAGE 30

Thunder Crashes
Anonymous

XIII

PAGE 32

The Pleiades
by Amy Lowell

XIV

PAGE 34

Tumbling
Anonymous

XV

PAGE 36

Happy as Kings
by Robert Louis Stevenson

Signs of Learning

American Sign Lanuage

 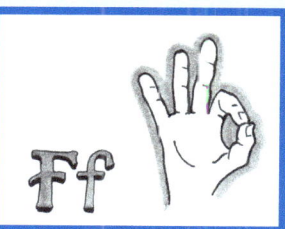  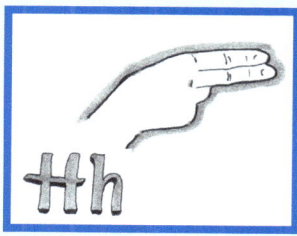

Poem

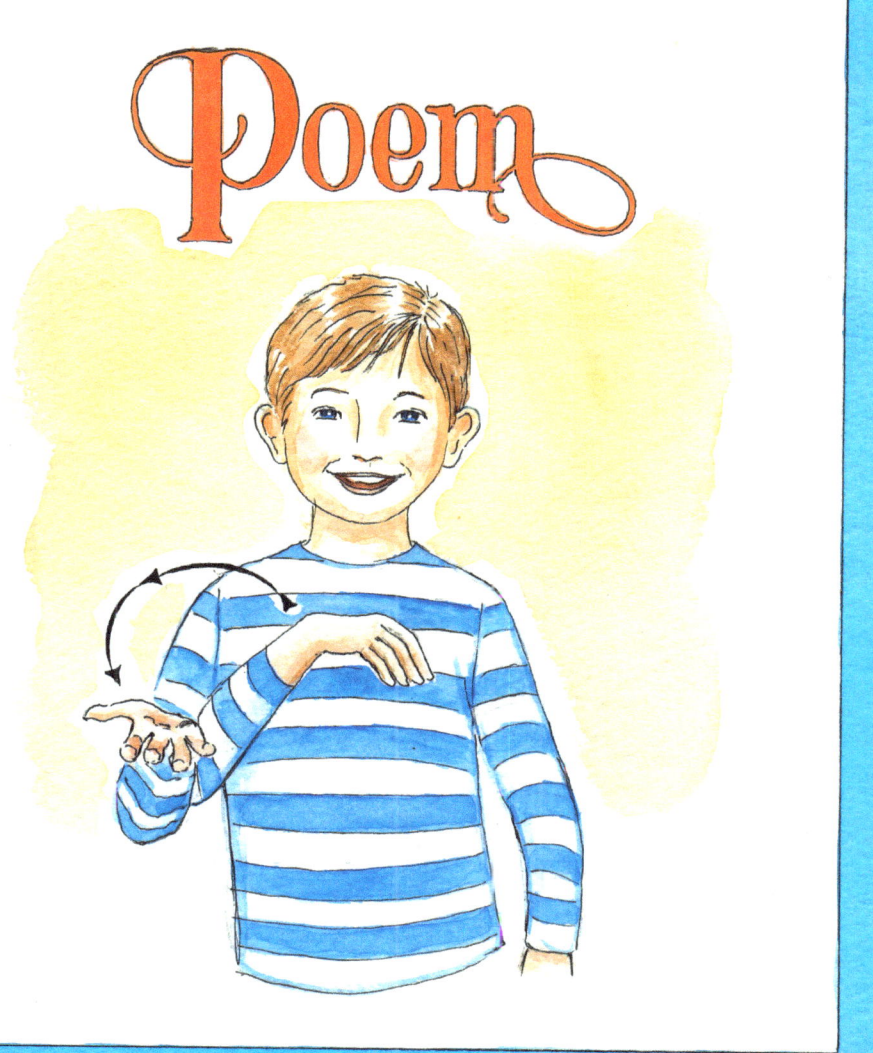

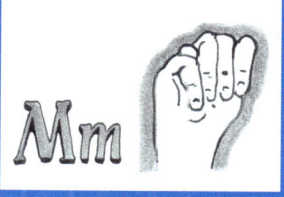

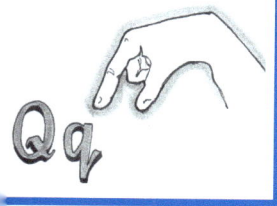  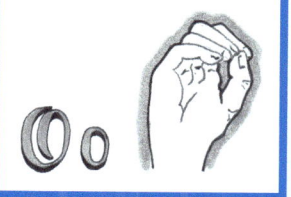 

Geese

Flag

Leaves

Sugar Plum

Hat

Bird

Swing

1 one 2 two 3 three

Counting and adding and subtracting are fun!

Shall we start with a four....4?
Shall we start with a one....1?

Or maybe a two....2?
Or could it be three....3?

You will know in a second what you want it to be!

seven 7 eight 8 nine 9

eleven 11
twelve 12

10
ten

9
nine

Can you be five?
.... 5?

Can you be two?
.... 2?

Look at the clock....

eight 8
seven 7

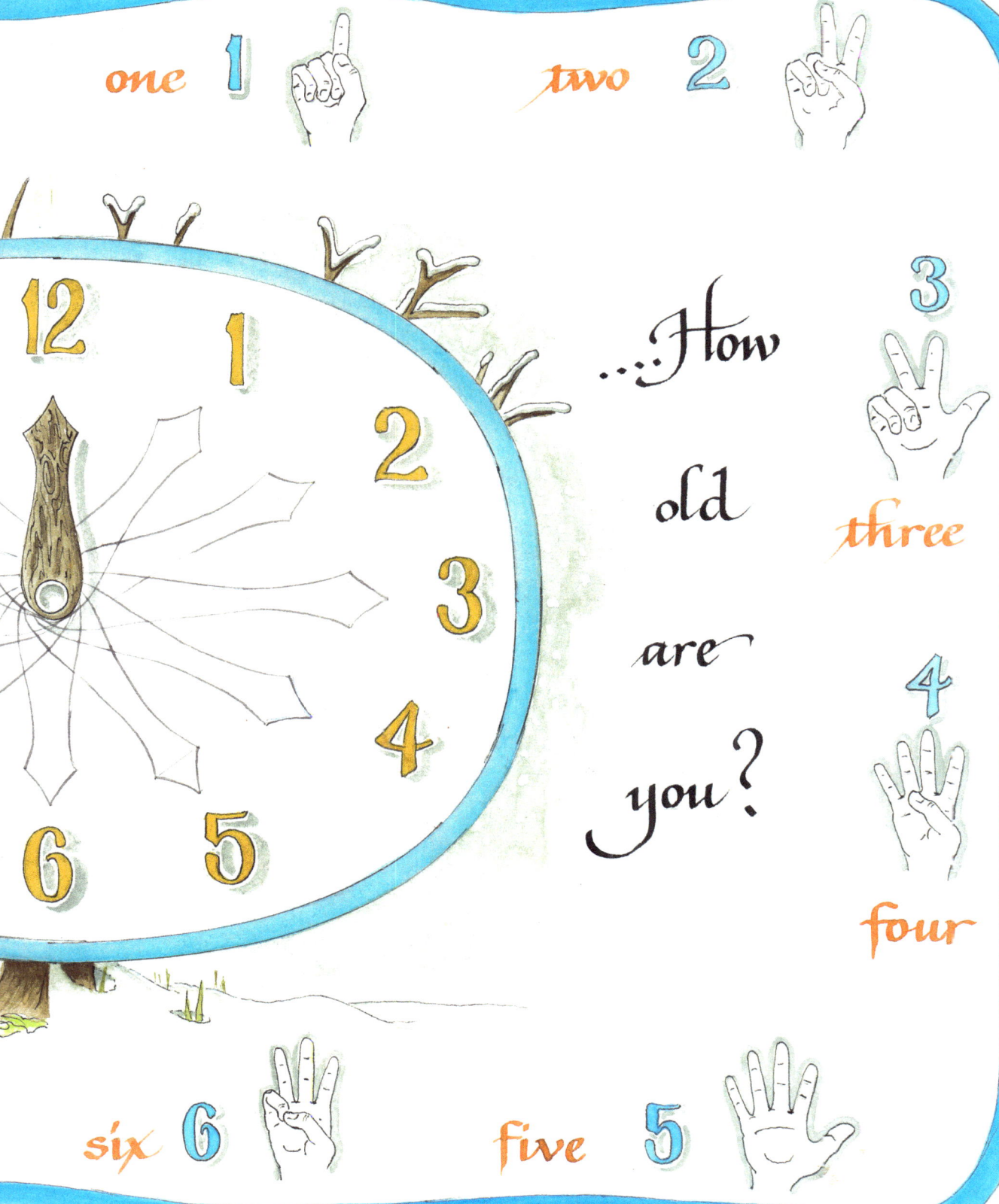

POEM

WELL DONE!

www.ingramcontent.com/pod-product-compliance
Lightning Source LLC
Chambersburg PA
CBHW042122040426
42450CB00002B/36